EASY GUITAR

Christmas Classics

ISBN 0-7935-6820-x

HAL•LEONARD®
CORPORATION

7777 W. BLUEMOUND RD. P.O. BOX 13819 MILWAUKEE, WI 53213

STRUM AND PICK PATTERNS

This chart contains the suggested strum and pick patterns that are referred to by number at the beginning of each song in this book. The symbols ⊓ and ∨ in the strum patterns refer to down and up strokes, respectively. The letters in the pick patterns indicate which right-hand fingers plays which strings.

p = thumb
i = index finger
m = middle finger
a = ring finger

For example; Pick Pattern 2
is played: thumb - index - middle - ring

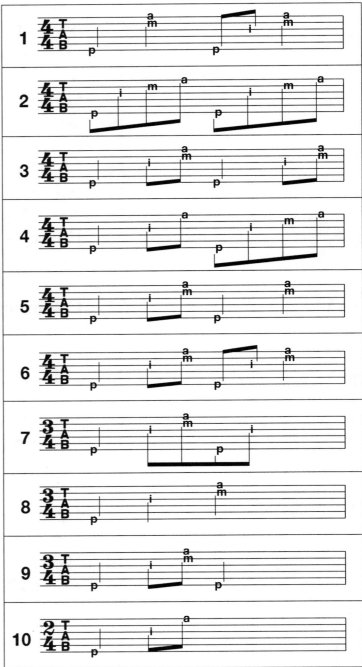

You can use the 3/4 Strum or Pick Patterns in songs written in compound meter (6/8, 9/8, 12/8, etc.). For example, you can accompany a song in 6/8 by playing the 3/4 pattern twice in each measure. The 4/4 Strum and Pick Patterns can be used for songs written in cut time (¢) by doubling the note time values in the patterns. Each pattern would therefore last two measures in cut time.

Auld Lang Syne

Words by Robert Burns
Traditional Melody

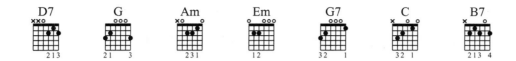

Strum Pattern: 3
Pick Pattern: 3

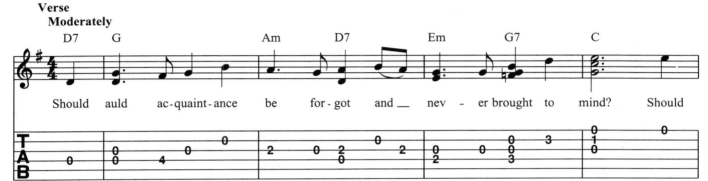

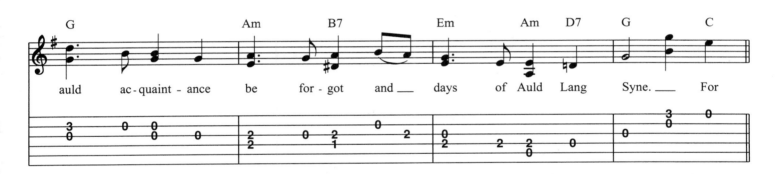

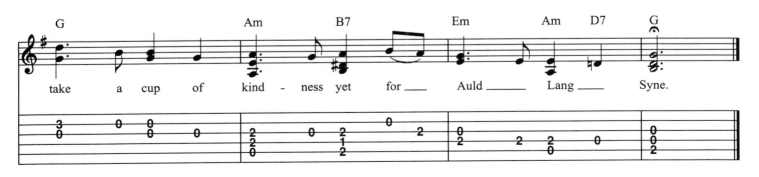

Angels We Have Heard on High

Traditional

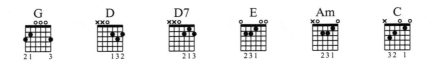

Strum Pattern: 6
Pick Pattern: 6

Verse
Moderately

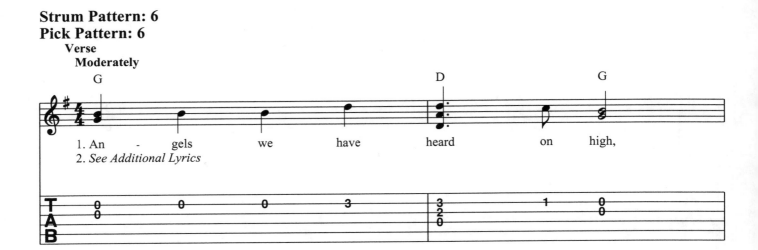

1. An - gels we have heard on high,
2. *See Additional Lyrics*

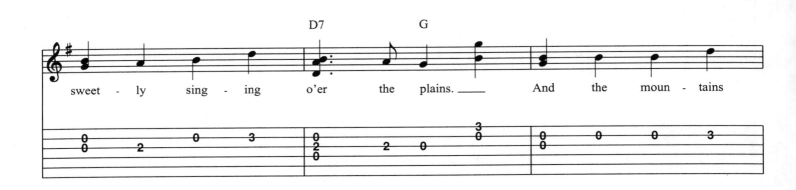

sweet - ly sing - ing o'er the plains. ___ And the moun - tains

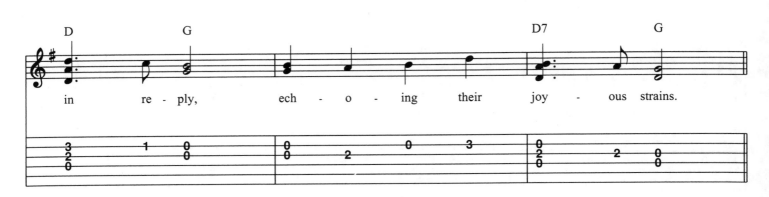

in re - ply, ech - o - ing their joy - ous strains.

Chorus

Glo -

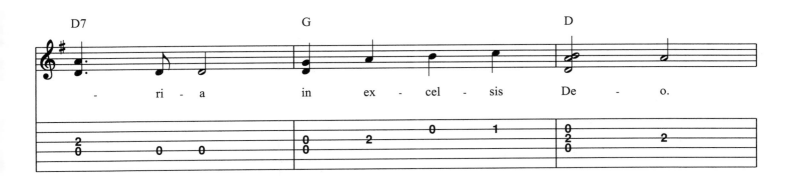

- ri - a in ex - cel - sis De - o.

Glo - ri - a

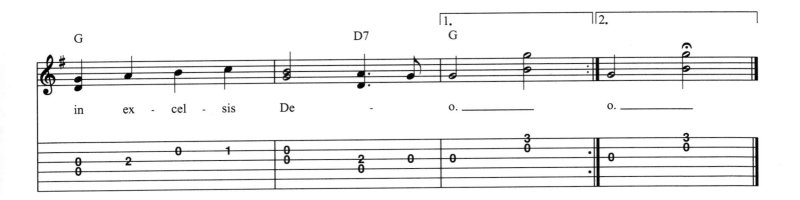

in ex - cel - sis De - o. o.

Additional Lyrics

2. Shepherds why this jubilee?
   Why your joyous strains prolong?
   What the gladsome tidings be
   Which inspire your heavenly song?

Ave Maria

By Franz Schubert

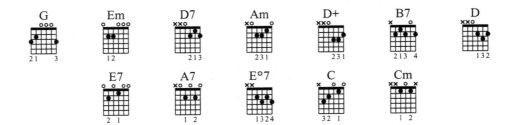

Strum Pattern: 1
Pick Pattern: 2

Verse
Reverently

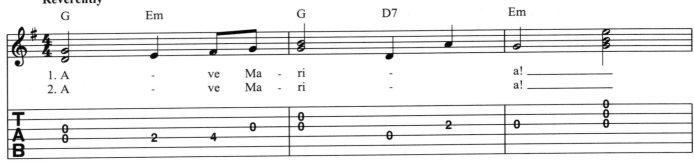

Bridge

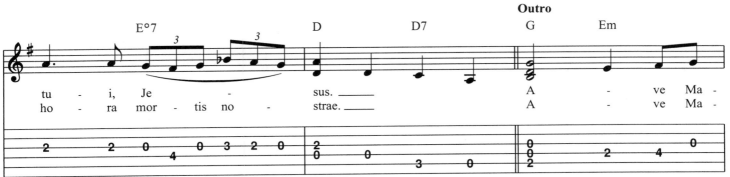

Outro

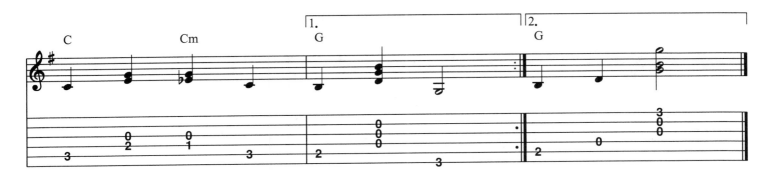

Away in a Manger

Words by Martin Luther
Music by Carl Mueller

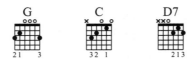

Strum Pattern: 9
Pick Pattern: 7

Verse
Sweetly

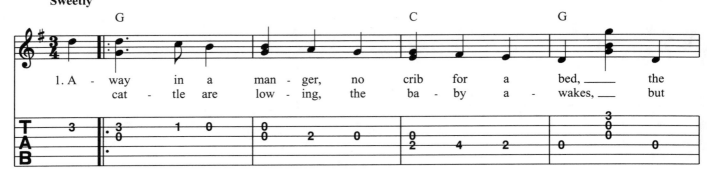

1. A - way in a man - ger, no crib for a bed, ___ the
cat - tle are low - ing, the ba - by a - wakes, ___ but

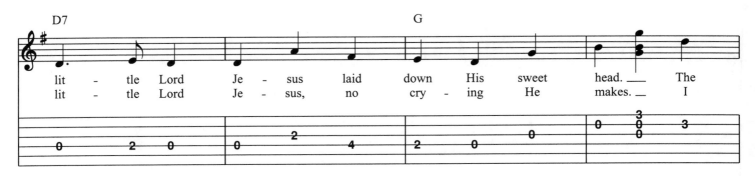

lit - tle Lord Je - sus laid down His sweet head. ___ The
lit - tle Lord Je - sus, no cry - ing sweet He makes. ___ I

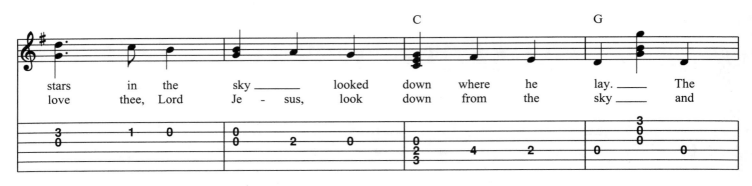

stars in the sky ___ looked down where he lay. ___ The
love thee, Lord Je - sus, look down from the sky ___ and

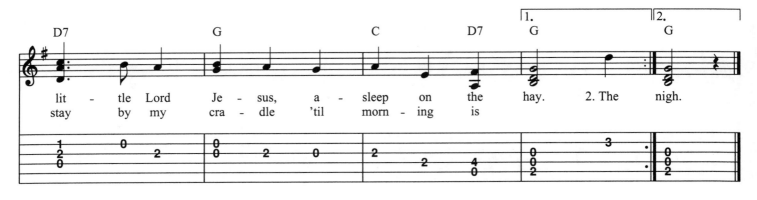

lit - tle Lord Je - sus, a - sleep on the hay. 2. The nigh.
stay by my cra - dle 'til morn - ing is

Deck the Hall

Traditional

Strum Pattern: 4, 6
Pick Pattern: 5, 6

Verse
Gaily

1. Deck the hall with boughs of hol - ly; fa, la, la, la, la, la, la, la, la.
2., 3. *See Additional Lyrics*

'Tis the sea - son to be jol - ly; fa, la, la, la, la, la, la, la, la.

Don we now our gay ap - par - el; fa, la, la, la, la, la, la, la, la. ____

Troll the an - cient yule - tide car - ol; fa, la, la, la, la, la, la, la, la. ____ la, la, la. ____

Additional Lyrics

2. See the blazing yule before us;
Fa, la, la, la, la, la, la, la, la.
Strike the harp and join the chorus;
Fa, la, la, la, la, la, la, la, la.
Follow me in merry measure;
Fa, la, la, la, la, la, la, la, la, la.
While I tell of Yuletide treasure;
Fa, la, la, la, la, la, la, la, la.

3. Fast away the old year passes;
Fa, la, la, la, la, la, la, la, la.
Hail the new ye lads and lasses;
Fa, la, la, la, la, la, la, la, la.
Sing we joyous, all together;
Fa, la, la, la, la, la, la, la, la.
Heedless of the wind and weather;
Fa, la, la, la, la, la, la, la, la.

The First Noël

Traditional

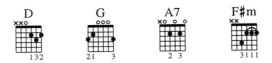

Strum Pattern: 7, 8
Pick Pattern: 8, 9

Verse
Moderately Slow

1. The __ first __ No - ël, the __ an - gel did say, was to
2.-5. *See Additional Lyrics*

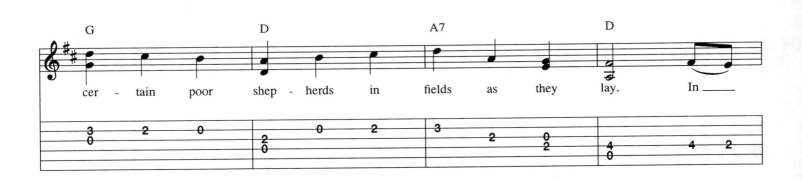

cer - tain poor shep - herds in fields as they lay. In _____

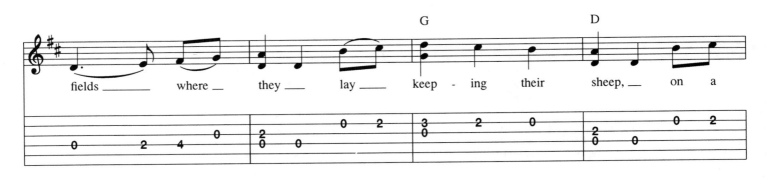

fields _____ where __ they __ lay _____ keep - ing their sheep, __ on a

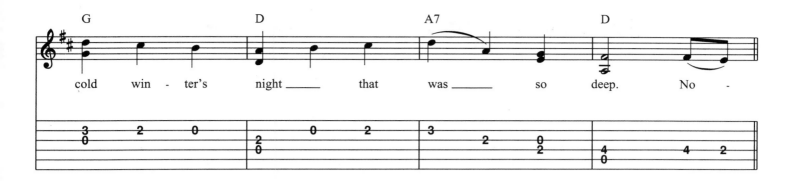

cold win - ter's night _____ that was _____ so deep. No -

Chorus

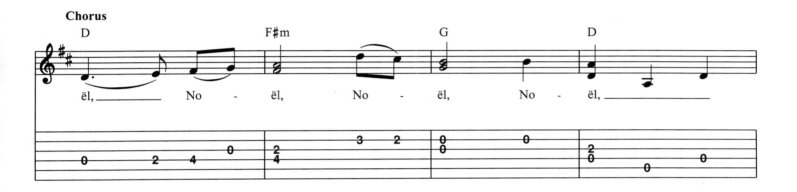

ël, _____ No - ël, No - ël, No - ël, _____

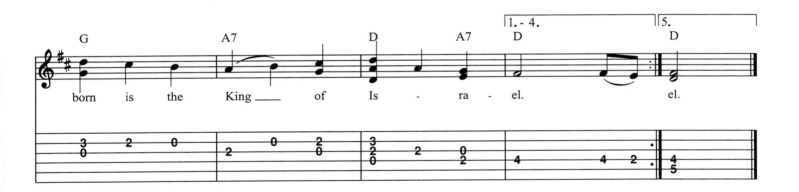

born is the King _____ of Is - ra - el. el.

Additional Lyrics

2. They looked up and saw a star
   Shining in the East, beyond them far.
   And to the earth it gave great light,
   And so it continued both day and night.

3. And by the light of that same star,
   Three wise man came from country far;
   To seek for a King was their intent,
   And to follow the star wherever it went.

4. This star drew nigh to the northwest,
   O'er Bethlehem it took its rest;
   And there it did both stop and stay,
   Right over the place where Jesus lay.

5. Then entered in those wise men three,
   Full reverently upon their knee;
   And offered there in His presence,
   Their gold and myrrh and frankincense.

God Rest Ye Merry, Gentlemen

Traditional

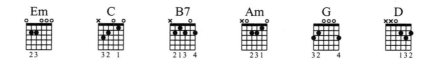

Strum Pattern: 3, 5
Pick Pattern: 3, 4

Verse
Moderately

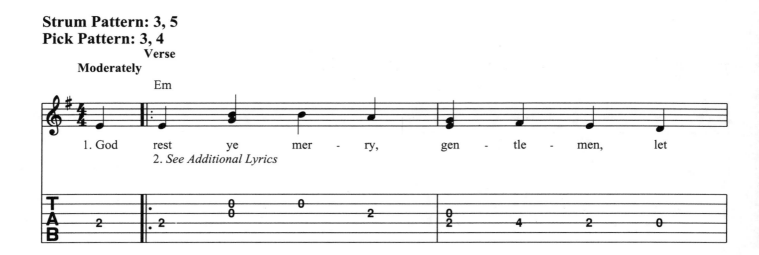

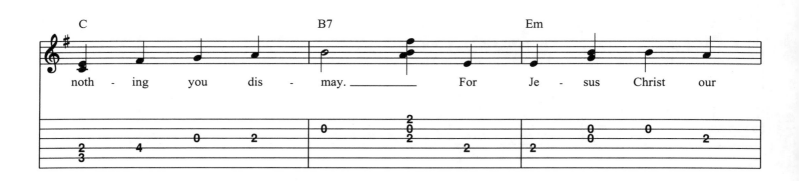

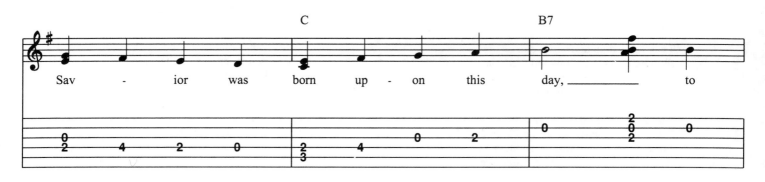

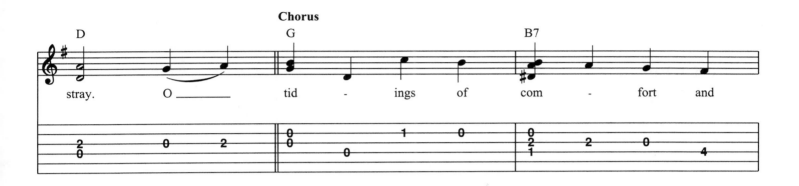

Chorus

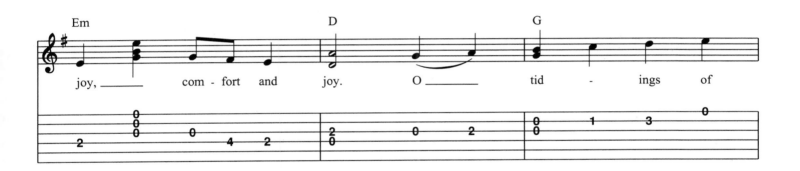

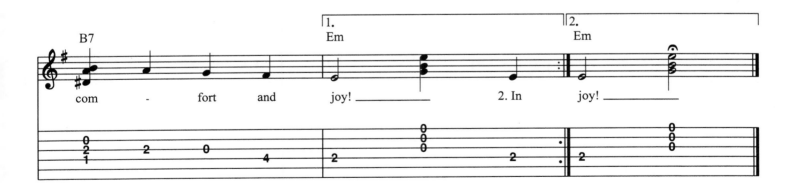

Additional Lyrics

2. In Bethlehem, in Jewry
This blessed babe was born
And laid within a manger
Upon this blessed morn
To which His mother Mary
Did nothing take in scorn.

Good King Wenceslas

Traditional

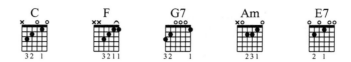

Strum Pattern: 3, 4
Pick Pattern: 3, 5

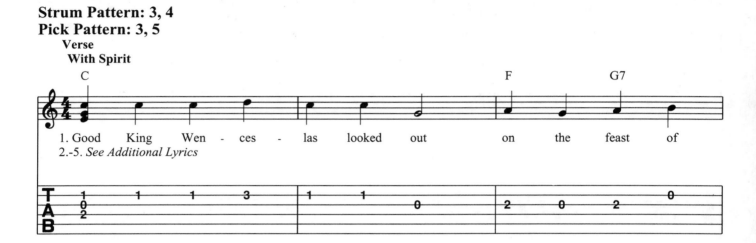

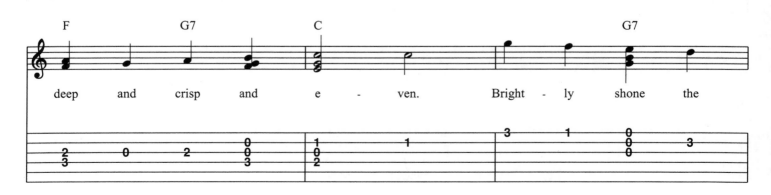

moon   that   night,   though   the   frost   was   cru - el;

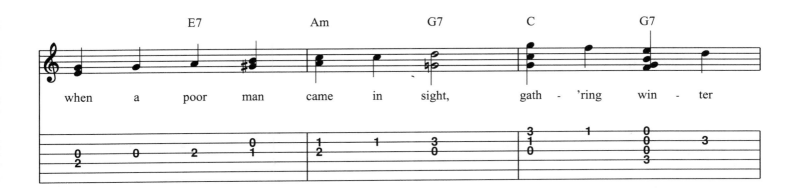

when   a   poor   man   came   in   sight,   gath - 'ring   win - ter

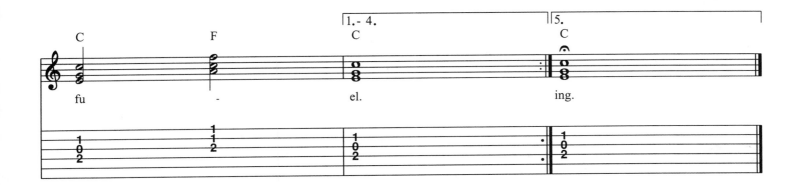

fu   -   el.   ing.

Additional Lyrics

2. "Hither page, and stand by me,
   If thou know'st it, telling;
   Yonder peasant, who is he?
   Where and what his dwelling?"
   "Sire, he lives a good league hence,
   Underneath the mountain;
   Right against the forest fence,
   By Saint Agnes' fountain."

3. "Bring me flesh, and bring me wine,
   Bring me pine-logs hither;
   Thou and I will see him dine,
   When we bear them thither."
   Page and monarch forth they went,
   Forth they went together;
   Through the rude winds wild lament,
   And the bitter weather.

4. "Sire, the night is darker now,
   And the wind blows stronger;
   Fails my heart, I know not how,
   I can go not longer."
   "Mark my footsteps, my good page,
   Tread thou in them boldly:
   Thou shalt find the winter's rage
   Freeze thy blood less coldly."

5. In his master's steps he trod,
   Where the snow lay dinted;
   Heat was in the very sod
   Which the saint has printed.
   Therefore, Christian men, be sure,
   Wealth or rank possessing;
   Ye who now will bless the poor,
   Shall yourselves find blessing.

Here We Come A-Wassailing

Traditional

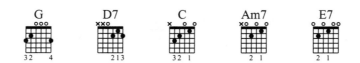

Strum Pattern: 8, 9
Pick Pattern: 7, 9

Verse
Brightly

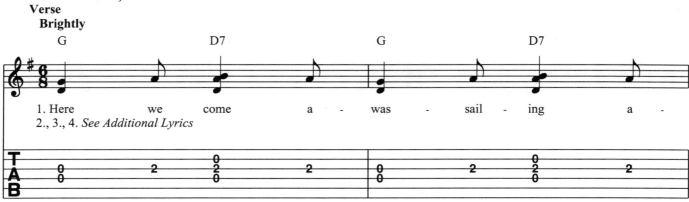

1. Here we come a - was - sail - ing a -
2., 3., 4. *See Additional Lyrics*

*Play patterns 2 times per measure for 6/8 only.

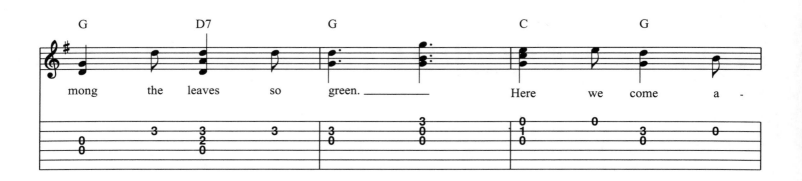

mong the leaves so green. _____ Here we come a -

Strum Pattern: 3
Pick Pattern: 3

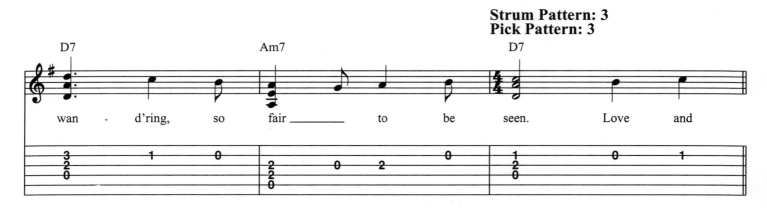

wan - d'ring, so fair _____ to be seen. Love and

Chorus

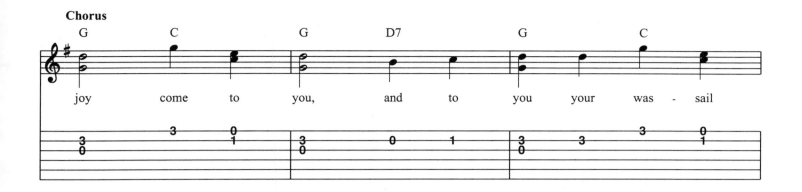

joy   come   to   you,   and   to   you   your   was - sail

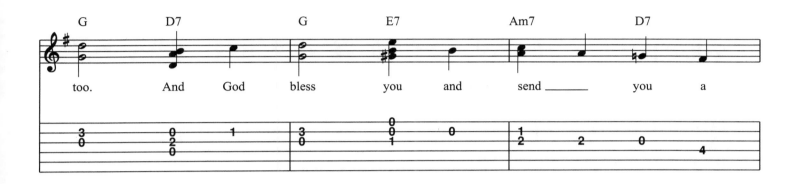

too.   And   God   bless   you   and   send _____   you   a

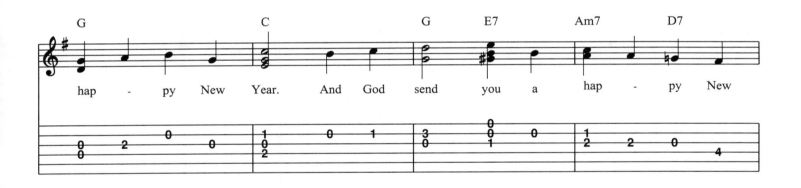

hap - py   New   Year.   And   God   send   you   a   hap - py   New

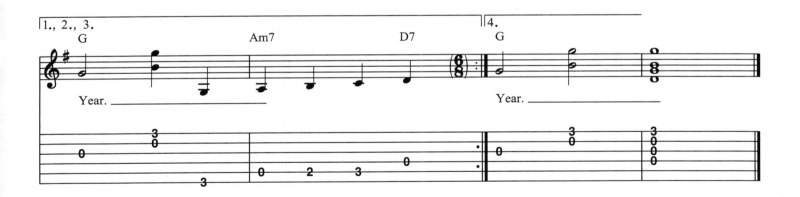

1., 2., 3.

Year. _____

4.

Year. _____

Additional Lyrics

2. We are not daily beggars
That beg from door to door.
But we are neighbor children
Whom you have seen before.

3. We have got a little purse
Of stretching leather skin.
We want a little money
To line it well within:

4. God bless the master of this house,
Likewise the mistress too;
And all the little children
That round the table go:

I Saw Three Ships

Tradional Irish Carol

*Strum Pattern: 7, 8
*Pick Pattern: 8, 9

Verse
Spirited

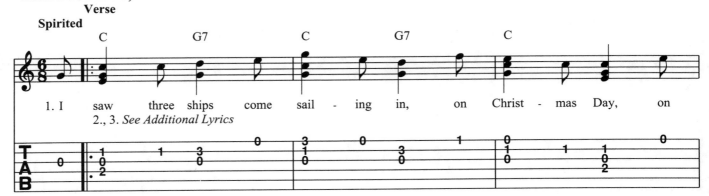

1. I saw three ships come sail - ing in, on Christ - mas Day, on
2., 3. *See Additional Lyrics*

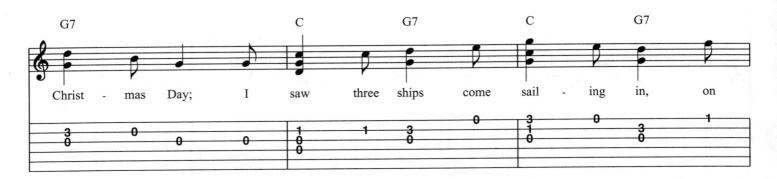

Christ - mas Day; I saw three ships come sail - ing in, on

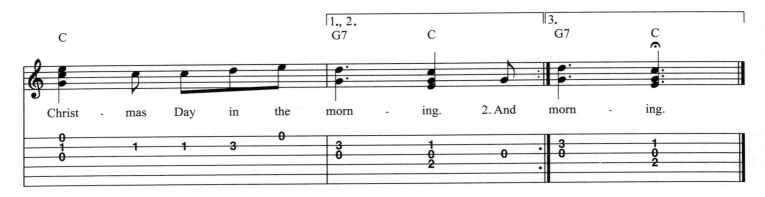

Christ - mas Day in the morn - ing. 2. And morn - ing.

Additional Lyrics

2. And what was in those ships, all three,
   On Christmas Day, on Christmas Day;
   And what was in those ships, all three,
   On Christmas Day in the morning?

3. The Virgin Mary and Christ were there,
   On Christmas Day, on Christmas Day;
   The Virgin Mary and Christ were there,
   On Christmas Day in the morning.

Jesus Holy, Born So Lowly

Traditional Polish

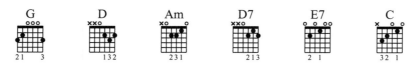

Strum Pattern: 8
Pick Pattern: 8

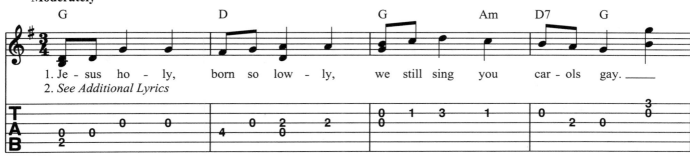

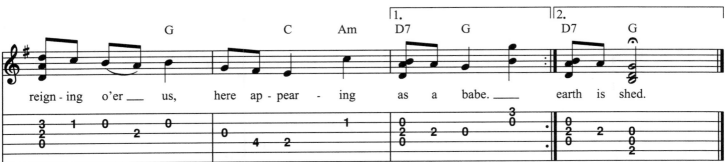

Additional Lyrics

2. On the straw the Babe is sleeping,
   In the humble manger bed.
   Mary loving watch is keeping,
   Angels hover 'round His head.
   Shepherds bow in adoration,
   Praising God's sweet benediction
   That upon the earth is shed.

It Came Upon the Midnight Clear

Words by Edmund H. Sears
Music by Richard Storrs Willis

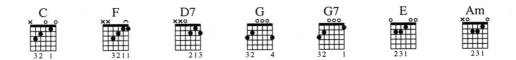

Strum Pattern: 7, 8
Pick Pattern: 8, 9

Verse
Quietly

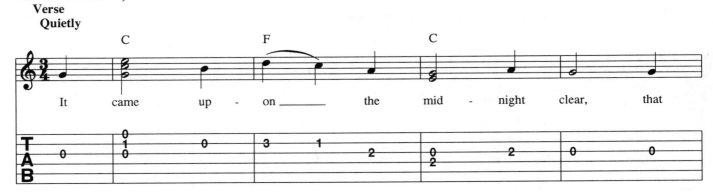

It came up - on _____ the mid - night clear, that

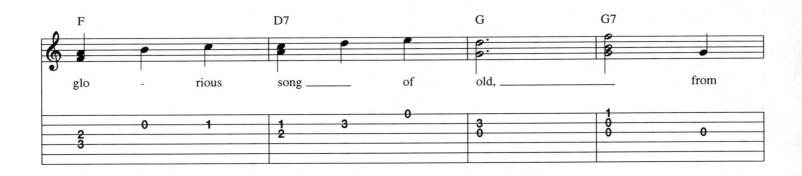

glo - rious song _____ of old, _____ from

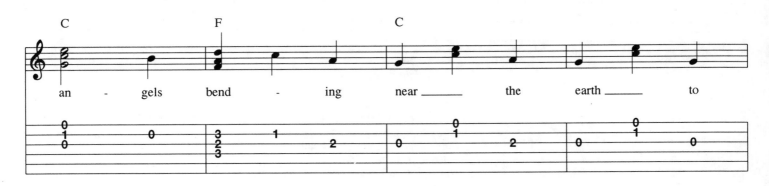

an - gels bend - ing near _____ the earth _____ to

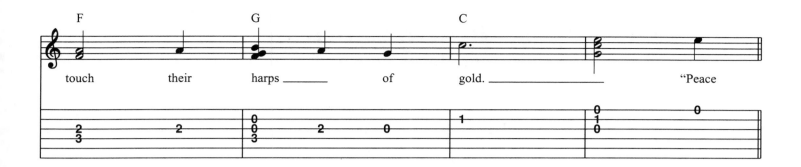

touch their harps ____ of gold. ____ "Peace

Bridge

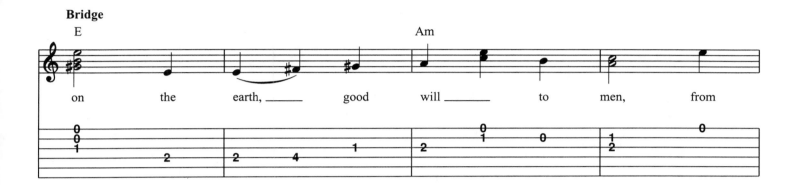

on the earth, ____ good will ____ to men, from

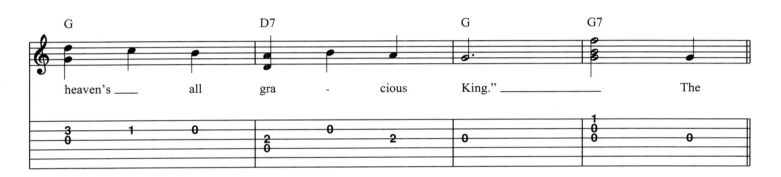

heaven's ____ all gra - cious King." ____ The

Outro

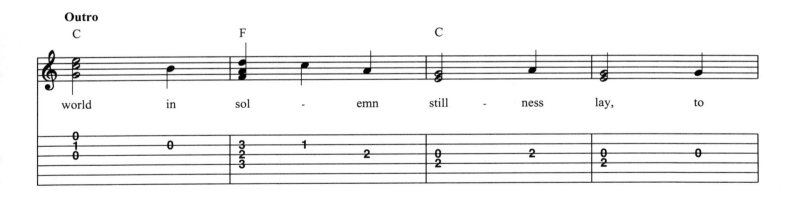

world in sol - emn still - ness lay, to

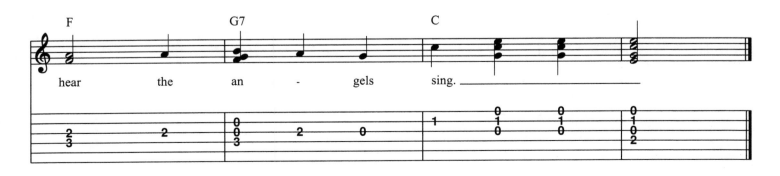

hear the an - gels sing. ____

Jingle Bells

Words and Music by J. Pierpont

Strum Pattern: 2, 3
Pick Pattern: 3, 4

Verse
Brightly

1. Dash - ing through the snow, _____ in a one horse o - pen sleigh, _____
2., 3. *See Additional Lyrics*

o'er the fields we go, laugh - ing all the way. _____

Bells on bob - tail ring, mak - ing spir - its bright. _____ What

fun it is to ride and sing a sleigh - ing song to - night! Oh!

Chorus

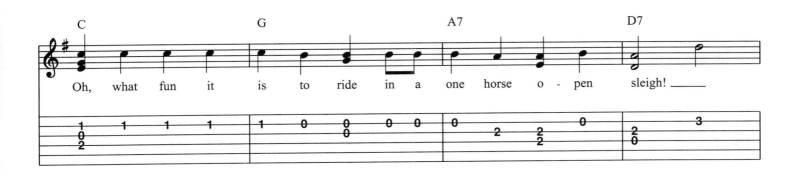

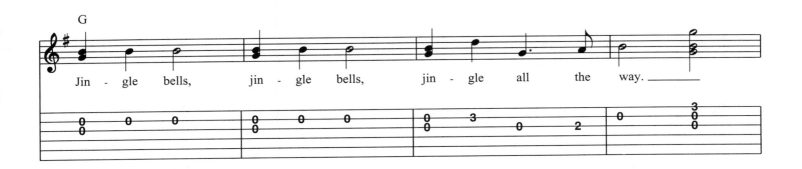

Additional Lyrics

2. A day or two ago, I thought I'd take a ride,
   And soon Miss Fannie Bright was sitting by my side.
   The horse was lean and lank,
   Misfortune seemed his lot.
   He got into a drifted bank and we, we got upshot! Oh!

3. Now the ground is white, go it while you're young.
   Take the girls tonight and sing this sleighing song.
   Just get a bobtail bay,
   Two-forty for his speed.
   Then hitch him to an open sleigh and
   Crack, you'll take the lead! Oh!

Jolly Old St. Nicholas

Traditional

Strum Pattern: 4
Pick Pattern: 4

Verse
Brightly

1. Jol - ly old Saint Nich - o - las, lean your ear this way. ___
2., 3. *See Additional Lyrics*

Don't you tell a sin - gle soul what I'm going to say. ___

Christ - mas Eve is com - ing soon, now, you dear old man, ___

whis - per what you'll bring to me; tell me if you can. ___ best. ___

Additional Lyrics

2. When the clock is striking twelve, when I'm fast asleep,
   Down the chimney broad and black, with your pack you'll creep.
   All the stockings you will find hanging in a row.
   Mine will be the shortest one, you'll be sure to know.

3. Johnny wants a pair of skates; Susy wants a sled.
   Nellie wants a picture book, yellow, blue and red.
   Now I think I'll leave to you what to give the rest.
   Choose for me, dear Santa Claus.
   You will know the best.

O Christmas Tree

Traditional

Strum Pattern: 7, 8
Pick Pattern: 8, 9

Verse
Moderately

1. O Christmas tree! O Christmas tree, you stand in verdant beauty! O
2., 3. *See Additional Lyrics*

Christmas tree, O Christmas tree, you stand in verdant beauty! Your

boughs are green in summer's glow, and do not fade in winter's snow. O

Christmas tree, O Christmas tree, you stand in verdant beauty! 2. O brightly. ___

Additional Lyrics

2. O Christmas tree! O Christmas tree,
   Much pleasure doth thou bring me!
   O Christmas tree! O Christmas tree,
   Much pleasure does thou bring me!
   For every year the Christmas tree
   Brings to us all both joy and glee.
   O Christmas tree, O Christmas tree,
   Much pleasure doth thou bring me!

3. O Christmas tree! O Christmas tree,
   Thy candles shine out brightly!
   O Christmas Tree, O Christmas tree,
   Thy candles shine out brightly!
   Each bough doth hold its tiny light
   That makes each toy to sparkle bright.
   O Christmas tree, O Christmas tree,
   Thy candles shine out brightly.

Joy to the World

Words by Isaac Watts
Music by George F. Handel

Strum Pattern: 3
Pick Pattern: 3

Verse
With Spirit

1. Joy to the World! The Lord is
2. *See Additional Lyrics*

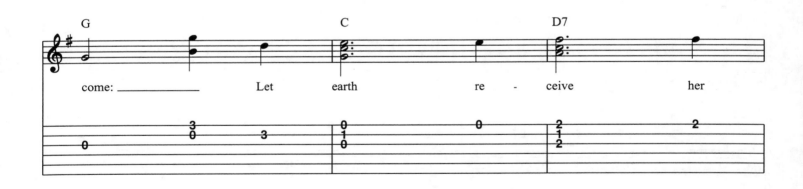

come: _____ Let earth re - ceive her

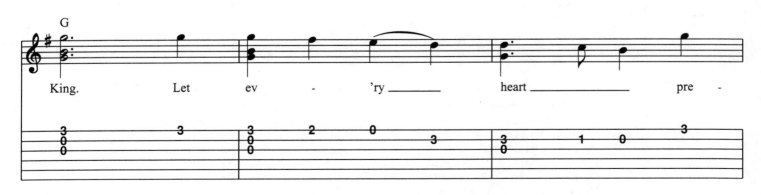

King. Let ev - 'ry _____ heart _____ pre -

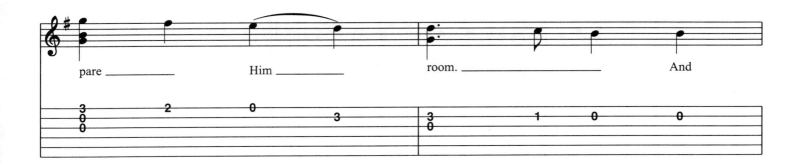

pare _____ Him _____ room. _____ And

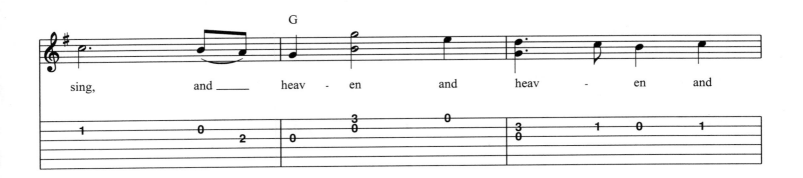

heav - en and na - ture ____ sing, and ____ heav - en and na - ture ____

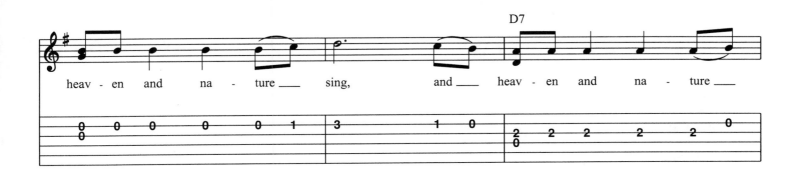

sing, and _____ heav - en and heav - en and

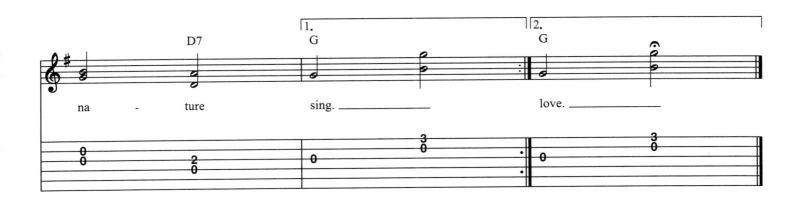

na - ture sing. _____ love. _____

Additional Lyrics

2. He rules the world with truth and grace
   And makes the nations prove
   The glories of His righteousness
   And wonders of His love,
   And wonders of His love,
   And wonders, wonders of His love.

O Come, All Ye Faithful
(Adeste Fidelis)

Traditional

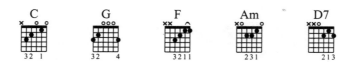

Strum Pattern: 4
Pick Pattern: 5

Verse
Triumphantly

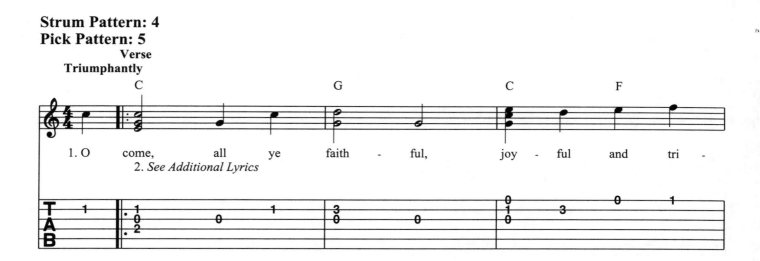

1. O come, all ye faith - ful, joy - ful and tri -

2. See Additional Lyrics

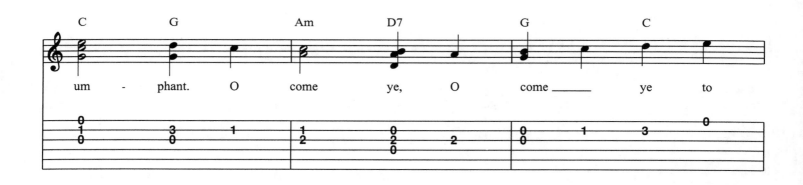

um - phant. O come ye, O come _____ ye to

Beth - le - hem; _____ Come and be -

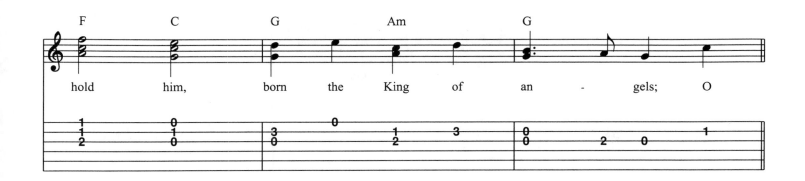

hold him, born the King of an - gels; O

Chorus

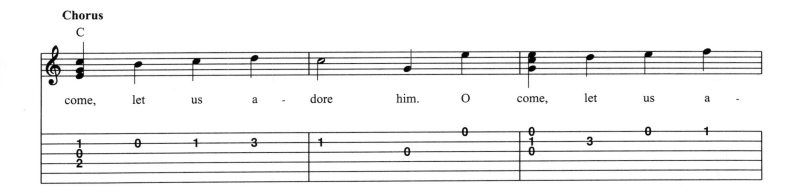

come, let us a - dore him. O come, let us a -

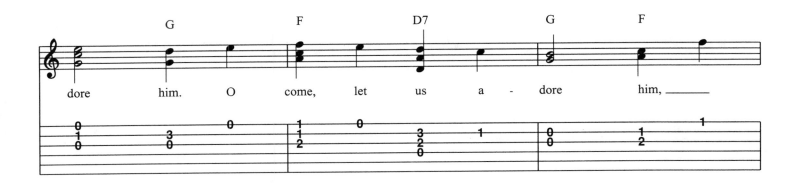

dore him. O come, let us a - dore him, _____

Christ, _____ the Lord! Lord!

Additional Lyrics

2. Sing choirs of angels, sing in exultation.
   O sing all ye citizens of heaven above.
   Glory to God in the highest.

O Holy Night

English Words by D.S. Dwight
Music by Adolphe Adam

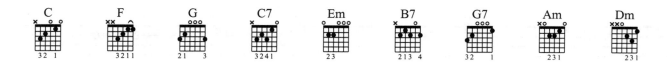

*Strum Pattern: 8, 9
*Pick Pattern: 8, 9

Verse

Slow And Flowing

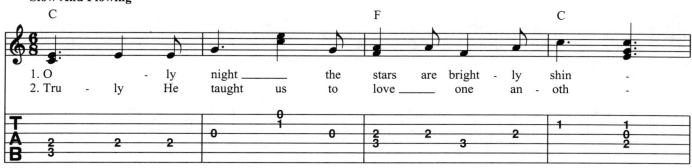

1. O - ly night _____ the stars are bright - ly shin -
2. Tru - ly He taught us to love _____ one an - oth -

*Play patterns 2 times per measure.

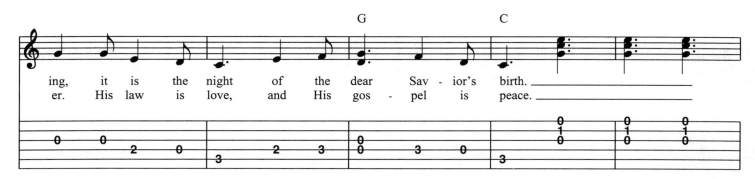

ing, it is the night of the dear Sav - ior's birth. _____
er. His law is love, and His gos - pel is peace. _____

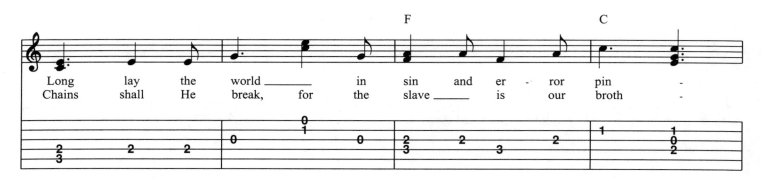

Long lay the world _____ in sin and er - ror pin -
Chains shall He break, for the slave _____ is our broth -

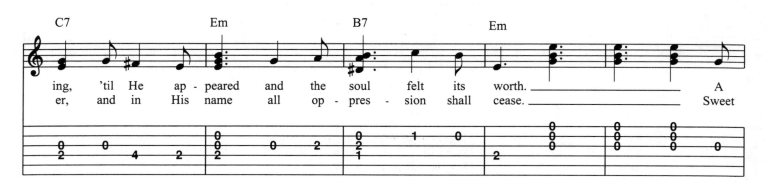

ing, 'til He ap - peared and the soul felt its worth. _____
er, and in His name all op - pres - sion shall cease. _____

A
Sweet

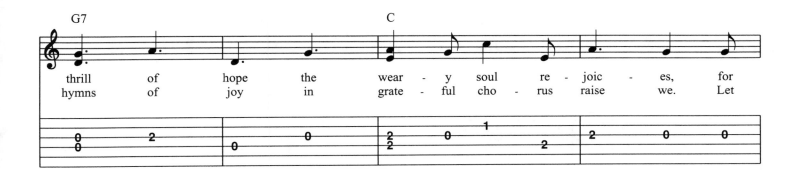

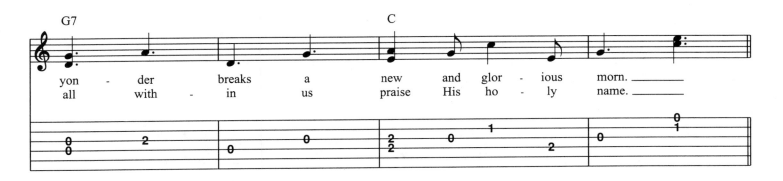

Chorus

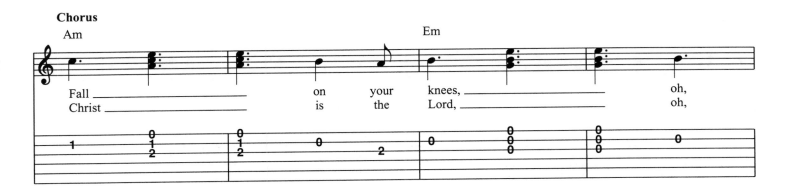

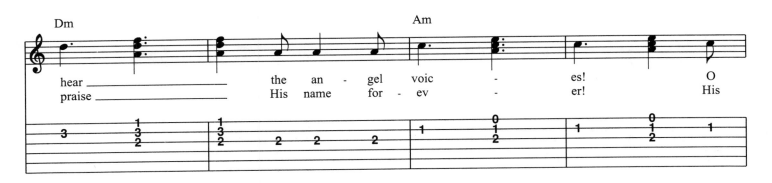

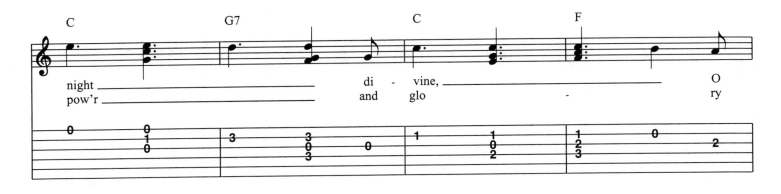

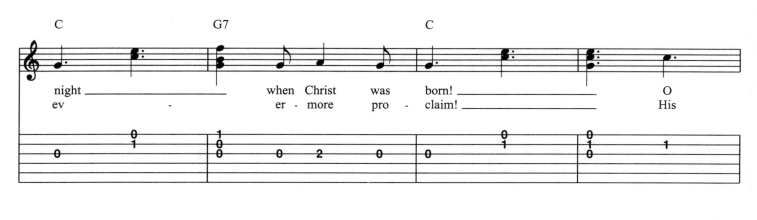

night _____ when Christ was born! _____ O

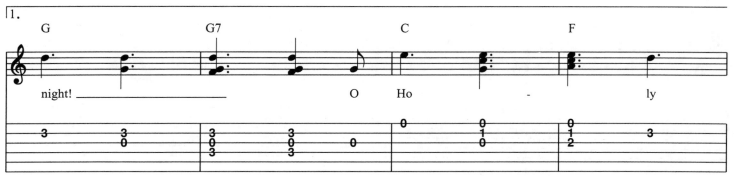

1.

night! _____ O Ho - ly

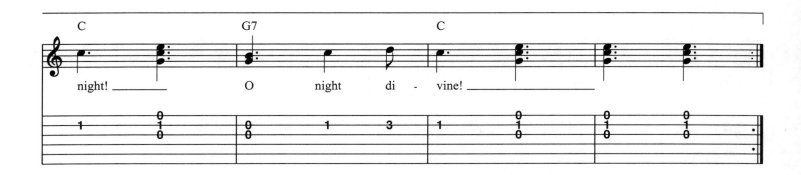

night! _____ O night di - vine! _____

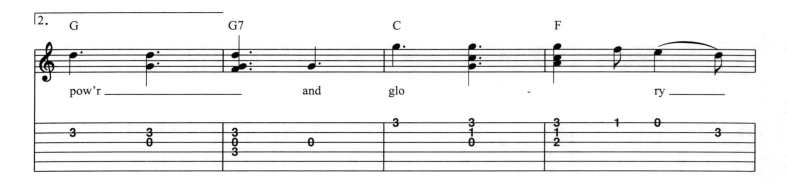

2.

pow'r _____ and glo - ry _____

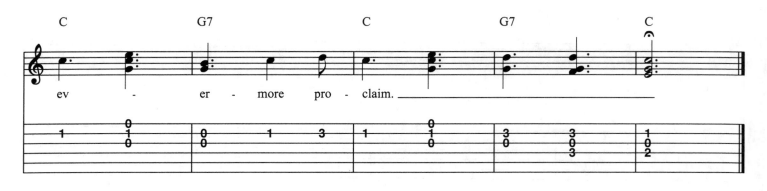

ev - er - more pro - claim. _____

O Little Town of Bethlehem

Traditional

Strum Pattern: 4
Pick Pattern: 5

Verse

Quietly

Additional Lyrics

2. For Christ is born of Mary, and gathered all above.
   While mortals sleep the angels keep
   Their watch of wond'ring love.
   O morning stars, together proclaim the holy birth!
   And praises sing to God the King,
   And peace to men on earth!

Once in Royal David's City

Words by C.F. Alexander
Music by Henry J. Gauntlett

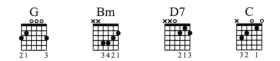

Strum Pattern: 4
Pick Pattern: 5

Verse
Quietly

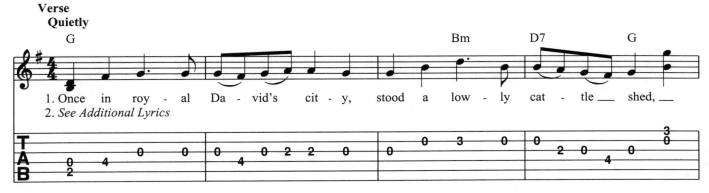

Additional Lyrics

2. And our eyes at last shall see Him,
   Through His own redeeming love.
   For that child so dear and gentle
   Is our Lord in heav'n above.
   And He leads His children on
   To the place where He is gone.

Pat-A-Pan
(Willie, Take Your Little Drum)

Words and Music by Bernard de la Monnoye

Strum Pattern: 2, 3
Pick Pattern: 2, 3

Additional Lyrics

2. When the men of olden days
Gave the King of Kings their praise,
They had pipes to play upon.
Tu-re-lu-re-lu, pat-a-pat-a-pan.
And also the drums they'd play.
Full of joy, on Christmas Day.

3. God and man today become
Closely joined as flute and drum.
Let the joyous tune play on!
Tu-re-lu-re-lu, pat-a-pat-a-pan.
As the instruments you play,
We will sing, this Christmas Day.

Silent Night

Words by Joseph Mohr
Music by Franz Gruber

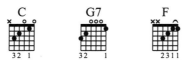

Strum Pattern: 7
Pick Pattern: 9

Verse
Quietly

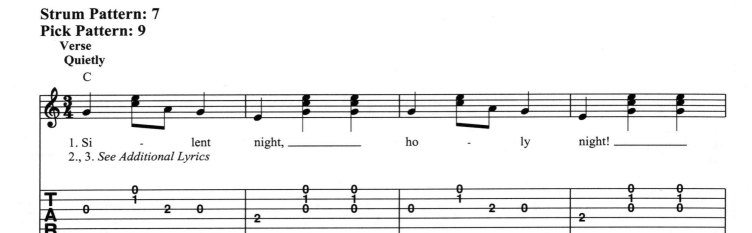

1. Si - lent night, _____ ho - ly night! _____
2., 3. *See Additional Lyrics*

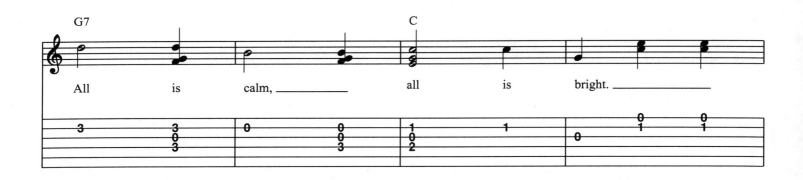

All is calm, _____ all is bright. _____

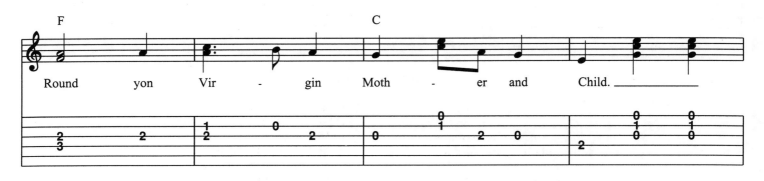

Round yon Vir - gin Moth - er and Child. _____

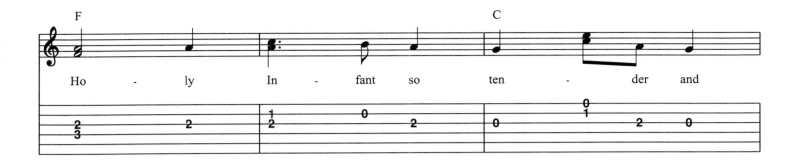

Ho - ly In - fant so ten - der and

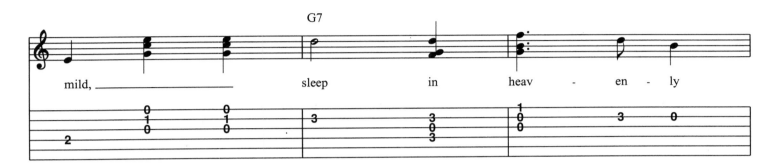

mild, _____ sleep in heav - en - ly

peace. _____ Sleep _____ in heav - en - ly

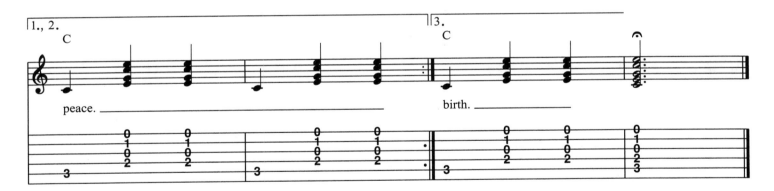

peace. _____ birth. _____

Additional Lyrics

2. Silent night, holy night!
   Shepherds quake at the sight.
   Glories stream from heaven afar.
   Heavenly hosts sing Alleluia.
   Christ the Savior is born!
   Christ the Savior is born!

3. Silent night, holy night!
   Son of God, love's pure light.
   Radiant beams from thy holy face
   With the dawn of redeeming grace.
   Jesus Lord at Thy birth.
   Jesus Lord at Thy birth.

Star of the East

Words by George Cooper
Music by Amanda Kennedy

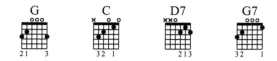

Strum Pattern: 9
Pick Pattern: 9

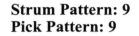

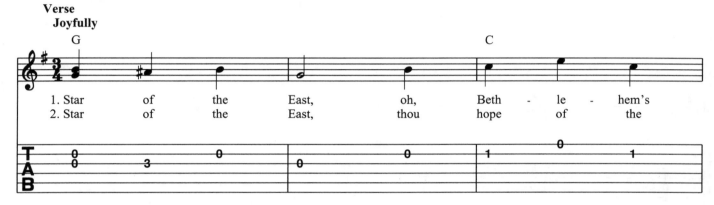

1. Star of the East, oh, Beth - le - hem's
2. Star of the East, oh, thou hope of the

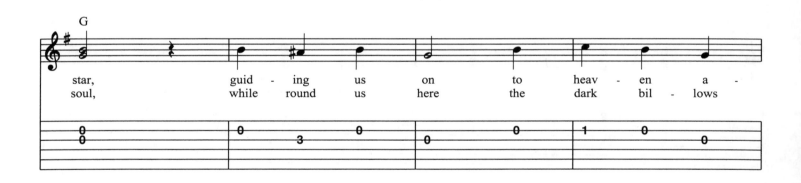

star, guid - ing us on to heav - en a -
soul, while round us on here to the dark en bil - lows

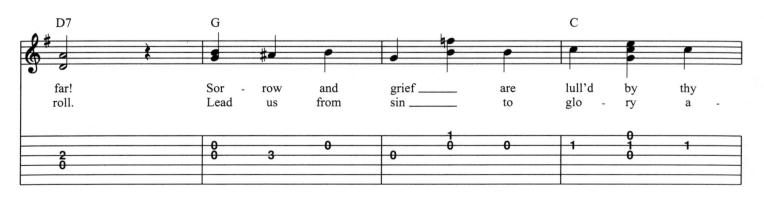

far! Sor - row and grief_____ are lull'd by thy
roll. Lead us and from sin_____ to glo - ry a -

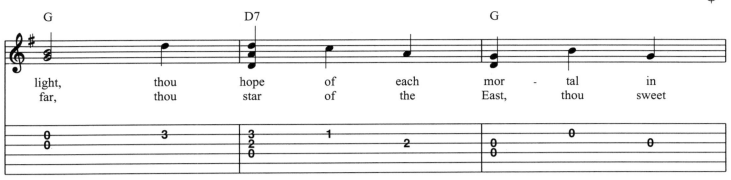

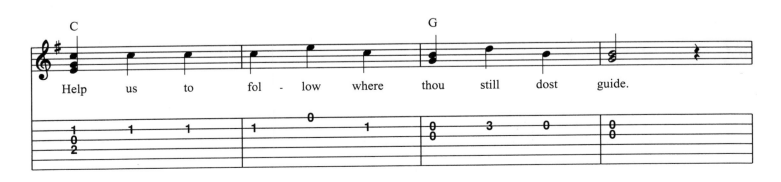

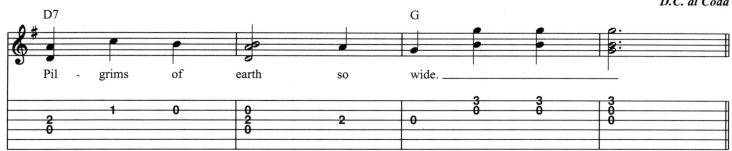

Pil - grims of earth so wide.

⊕ *Coda*

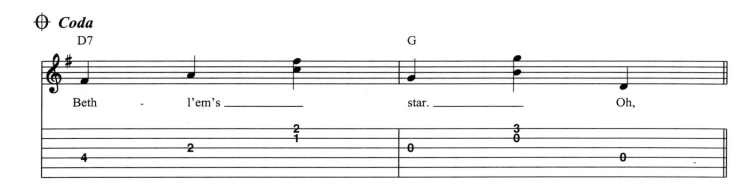

Beth - l'em's _____ star. _____ Oh,

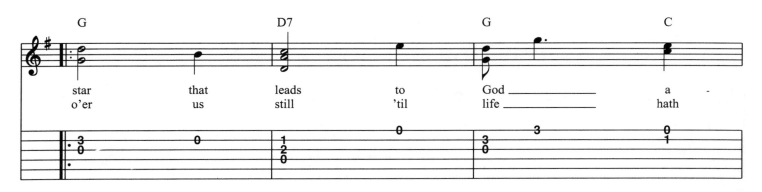

star that leads to God _____ a -
o'er us still 'til life _____ hath

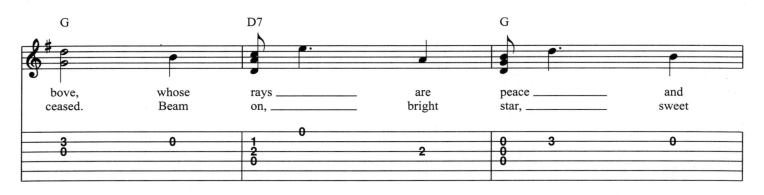

bove, whose rays _____ are peace _____ and
ceased. Beam on, _____ bright star, _____ and sweet

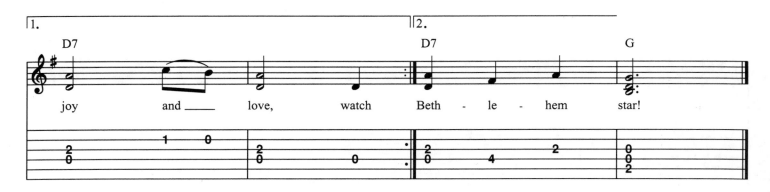

joy and _____ love, watch Beth - le - hem star!

Up on the Housetop

Traditional

Strum Pattern: 3, 4
Pick Pattern: 3, 5

Additional Lyrics

2. First comes the stocking of Little Nell,
   Oh, dear Santa, fill it well.
   Give her a dollie that laughs and cries,
   One that will open and shut her eyes.

'Twas the Night Before Christmas

Words by Clement Clark Moore
Music by F. Henri Klickman

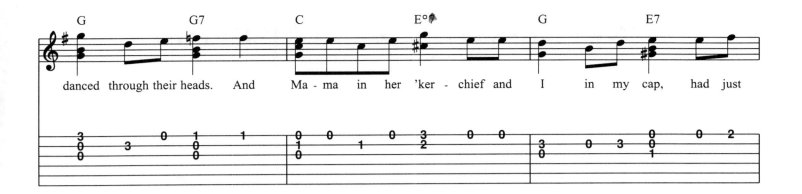

danced through their heads. And Ma - ma in her 'ker - chief and I in my cap, had just

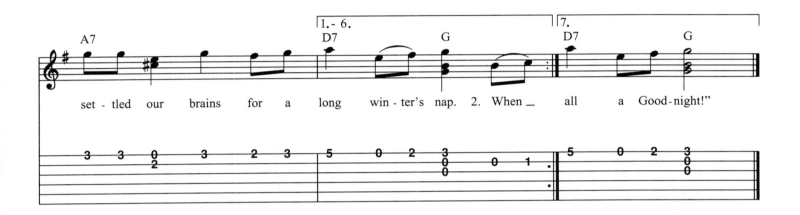

set - tled our brains for a long win - ter's nap. 2. When ___ all a Good-night!"

Additional Lyrics

2. When out on the lawn there arose such a clatter;
   I sprang from my bed to see what was the matter.
   Away to the window I flew like a flash,
   Tore open the shutters and threw up the sash.
   The moon, on the breast of the new-fallen snow,
   Gave a lustre of midday to objects below.
   When what to my wondering eyes should appear
   But a miniature sleigh and eight tiny reindeer.

3. With a little old driver, so lively and quick,
   I knew in a moment it must be Saint Nick.
   More rapid than eagles, his coursers they came
   And he whistled and shouted and called them by name:
   "Now, Dasher, Now, Dancer! Now, Prancer! Now, Vixen!
   On Comet! On, Cupid! On Donner and Blitzen!
   To the top of the porch, to the top of the wall!
   Now dash away, dash away, dash away all!"

4. As dry leaves that before the wild hurricane fly,
   When they meet with an obstacle, mount to the sky.
   So up to the house-top the coursers they flew,
   With the sleigh full of toys and Saint Nicholas, too.
   And then in a twinkling I heard on the roof
   The prancing and pawing of each little hoof.
   As I drew in my head, and was turning around,
   Down the chimney Saint Nicholas came with a bound.

5. He was dressed all in fur from his head to his foot
   And his clothes were all tarnished with ashes and soot.
   A bundle of toys he had flung on his back
   And he looked like a peddler just opening his pack.
   His eyes how they twinkled! His dimples how merry!
   His cheeks were like roses, his nose like a cherry,
   His droll little mouth was drawn up like a bow
   And the beard of his chin was as white as the snow.

6. The stump of a pipe he held tight in his teeth
   And the smoke, it encircled his head like a wreath.
   He had a broad face and a round little belly
   That shook, when he laughed, like a bowl full of jelly.
   He was chubby and plump, a right jolly old elf,
   And I laughed when I saw him, in spite of myself.
   A wink of his eye and a twist of his head,
   Soon gave me to know I had nothing to dread.

7. He spoke not a word but went straight to his work
   And filled all the stockings, then turned with a jerk,
   And laying his finger aside of his nose,
   And giving a nod, up the chimney he rose.
   He sprang to his sleigh, to his team gave a whistle
   And away they all flew like the down of a thistle.
   But I heard him exclaim, 'ere he drove out of sight:
   "Happy Christmas to all, and to all a Good-night!"

We Three Kings of Orient Are

Words and Music by John H. Hopkins

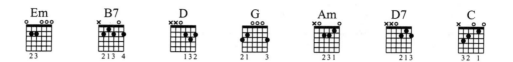

Strum Pattern: 8
Pick Pattern: 8

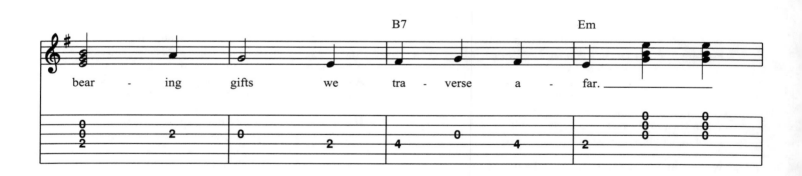

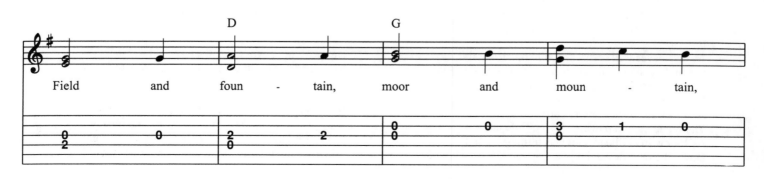

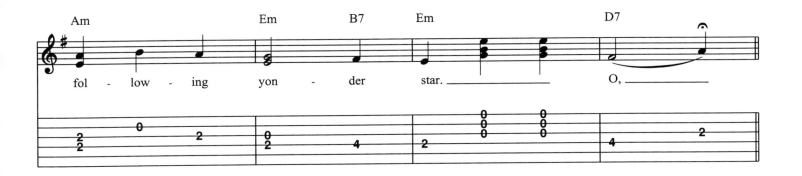

Chorus

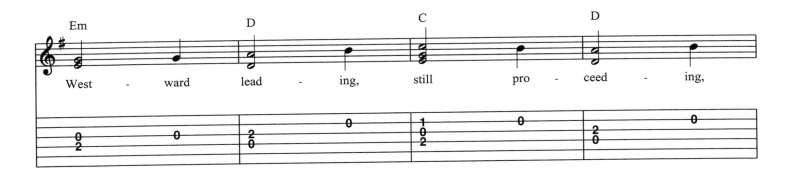

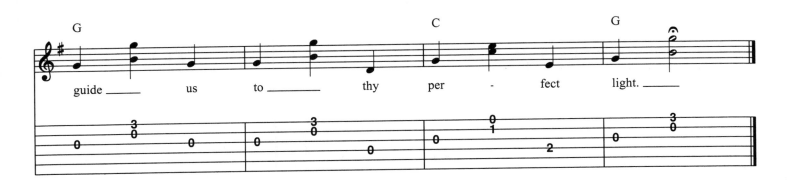

What Child Is This?

Traditional

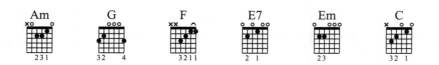

Strum Pattern: 7, 8
Pick Pattern: 8, 9

Verse

Slowly

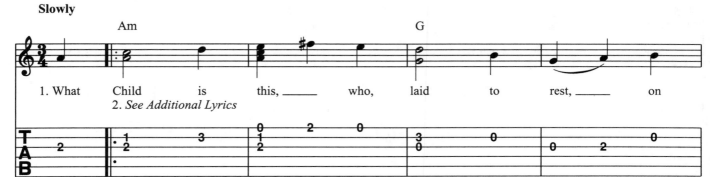

1. What Child is this, _____ who, laid to rest, _____ on
2. *See Additional Lyrics*

Ma - ry's lap _____ is sleep - ing? Whom

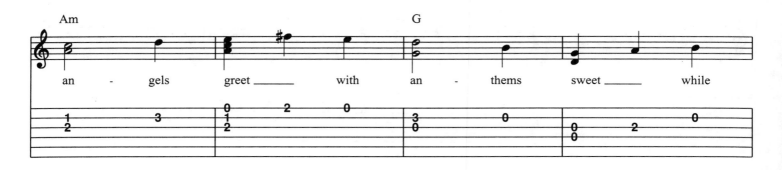

an - gels greet _____ with an - thems sweet _____ while

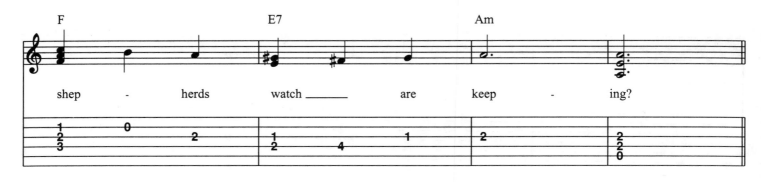

shep - herds watch _____ are keep - ing?

Chorus

This, this _____ is Christ the King, _____ whom

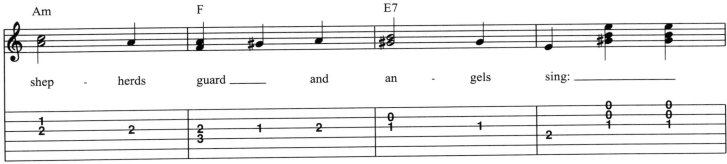

shep - herds guard _____ and an - gels sing: _____

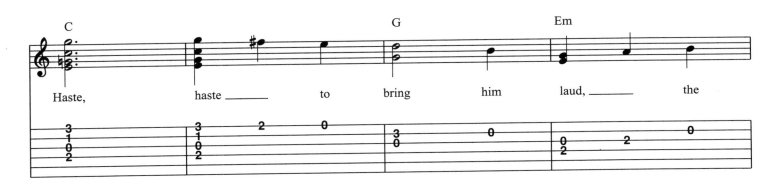

Haste, haste _____ to bring him laud, _____ the

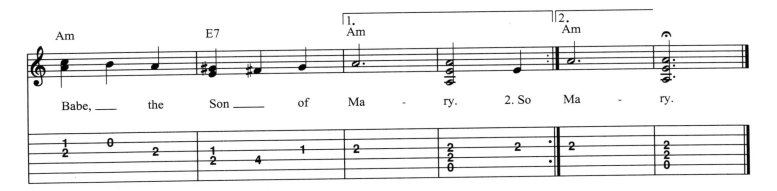

Babe, _____ the Son _____ of Ma - ry. 2. So Ma - ry.

Additional Lyrics

2. So bring Him incense, gold and myrrh,
   Come peasant king to own Him;
   The King of kings salvation brings.
   Let loving hearts enthrone Him.

Chorus   Raise, raise the song on high,
   The Virgin sings her lullaby;
   Joy, joy for Christ is born,
   The Babe, the Son of Mary.

We Wish You a Merry Christmas

Traditional

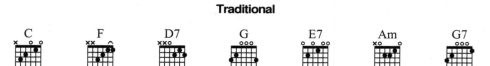

Strum Pattern: 8, 9
Pick Pattern: 8, 9

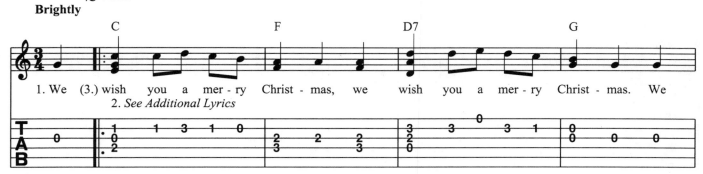

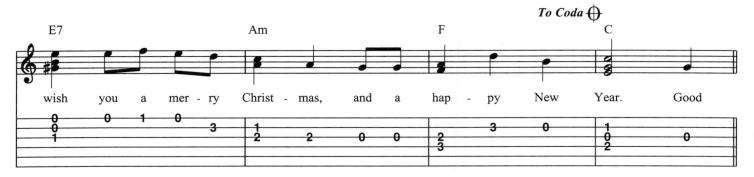

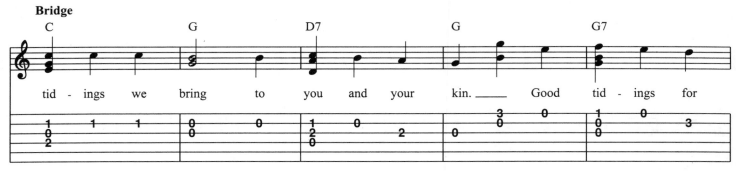

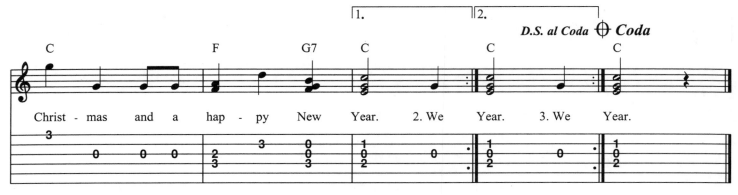

Additional Lyrics

2. We all know that Santa's coming.
   We all know that Santa's coming.
   We all know that Santa's coming
   And soon will be here.